ISLAM
Does It Make Sense?

Third edition

Printed in Canada

ISBN 0-9734601-0-5

ISLAM
Does It Make Sense?

Ayub A. Hamid

Third Edition

Bayaan Communications and Publications
Ontario, Canada

www.bayaanpublications.com

Dedicated to those who are blessed with:

- *the vision to seek the Truth*
- *the wisdom to recognize it*
- *the willingness to adopt it*
- *the courage to live by it*

FOREWORD

$\mathcal{T}$his is the third edition of *"Islam – Does It Make Sense"* which evolved from my attempts in the early nineties to introduce my non-Muslim colleagues to Islam and its common sense approach to matters of faith. When I shared my initial brief "Introduction to Islam" document with them, I realized that there was a communication gap between us: I was looking at the religion from a logical point of view with a mindset that the beliefs of a person should make sense. They were assuming that faith must be blind and that it should not have to make sense. Obviously, this gap required bridging with more explanations and examples, which gradually took the shape of this booklet.

The contents of this booklet are intended neither to be a profound thesis in philosophy nor does it indulge in deep philosophical discussions. It simply uses a commonsense approach to matters of faith for the benefit of the average person. The intent is merely to show why I think that faith should make sense and how I think Islam makes the most sense. This has been written especially for those who:

- *Like to take a rational approach to issues in life and religion;*
- *Prefer logical thinking rather than blind faith; and,*
- *Want to make their own decisions based on knowledge and intelligence rather than adopting society's decisions by default.*

If you are endowed with any of these attributes, you will enjoy the rational approach of this booklet and its presentation of basic realities of faith in a straightforward manner. It aims to present the essence of religious thought logically, unencumbered by illogical dogmas of theology and the emotional baggage of preachers.

To derive maximum benefit from this booklet, please free yourself from any pre-conceived notions that you may have about religion in general and Islam in particular. Please approach its study with an open mind, ready to accept what makes sense.

The feedback from those who were able to read the first two editions has been very encouraging. Readers sent appreciative notes and comments. Some located my phone number to personally communicate their enthusiasm and appreciation for the book. People acquired multiple copies to give to their friends and colleagues. Muslim converts found it very helpful to strengthen the foundations of their new faith and to introduce Islam to their family and friends.

The most gratifying aspect of the booklet has been its impact on Muslim youth. It has helped them rediscover and make sense of their faith in a way they can relate to and understand. It has helped them establish their religious beliefs on a firm intellectual foundation, rather than blindly accepting what their parents taught them.

This booklet reached the present stage only with the help, support, reviews, comments and feedback from my son, Omair M. Hamid of Toronto, Ontario, and Ashmede Asgarali of Winnipeg, Manitoba as well as sustained understanding and support of my wife, Zahida.

I sincerely hope that this booklet will assist you in developing a better understanding of Islamic beliefs. If you have further questions, please feel free to contact me at **ayubhamid@yahoo.ca**.

Ayub Azhar Hamid
October 5, 2005

CONTENTS

$Chapter$ 1

Humankind, Universe and God

EVERY human being, consciously or unconsciously, believes in and follows a religious philosophy. By the term "religious philosophy" I mean the belief, view or opinion of a person about the reality of human life, of universe, of God, and of the relationship that should exist among these entities. People believe in one God (monotheism), many gods (polytheism), or no god (atheism). Some people do not know what to make of God or do not care (agnosticism). Even the concept of God itself varies greatly among people who believe in some kind of deity.

All human beings, however, have one of these views through which they see the world and interpret various things in life. This view, belief or paradigm determines, to a large extent, their philosophy, approach and outlook towards life. In other words, every person's way of life is based upon the philosophy that emanates from their belief about God and their view of the relationships among God, humanity and the universe. For example, people who believe in some kind of God will try to live the way their God will be pleased with or approve of. Depending on the concept of God in one's mind, that lifestyle will differ. Atheists or agnostics will live a life according to their own whims and desires or society's default standards, usually resulting in a focus on maximizing the pleasures of this life and fulfillment of their wishes. Thus, maximizing the satisfaction of desires becomes their objective, religious philosophy or "god". Hence, whether a person is religious in common terms or an atheist, communist or agnostic, everyone has a religious philosophy to live by. One's religious philosophy, as such, has a profound, overall impact on every aspect of one's life, throughout one's life.

People adopt their religious philosophies by choice or by default. Some people think, study, challenge and, after some sort of critique and evaluation, choose a religious philosophy. The depth and breadth of their thinking, evaluation, critique or research varies, but the adoption of a particular philosophy becomes their own conscious decision. Others do not give much thought to philosophical matters and usually end up having chosen for them, by default, their family religion or prevalent philosophies, theories and norms of the society around them. By failing to pay due attention, they let other people make decisions for them.

Since the religious view or philosophy has such a significant impact on a person's life, it must be adopted after careful consideration and due diligence. After all, only one of the religious views is in fact accurate. Truth has only one version. Any other version may be right or wrong in various degrees. It may be substantially right, partly right, partly wrong, substantially wrong or absolutely wrong, etc. but only one version can be totally right. So it is incumbent on every one of us to try our utmost to find the truth to the best of our ability. Certainly it is difficult and no doubt different people will reach different conclusions, but at least they must try to find the truth for themselves. When we do not pay serious attention to consciously choosing a course, we are letting chance determine it for us. When we follow the popular ideas of society without evaluating them critically, we are letting other people make decisions for us. But it is our life. We must make our own decisions and set our own directions. Something with such far-reaching implications cannot be left to chance or relegated to other people to decide for us. If other people conclude differently from us, and no doubt many will, we must respect their right and privilege to make their own choices and tolerate generously and graciously their lifestyles, but we must never give up our own right to chart our own course.

One prerequisite to making an appropriate decision is to think rationally. When it comes to anything related to religious matters, people often react emotionally rather than thinking rationally. Also, most "religious people" believe blindly. They do not want to evaluate their religious faith rationally. They think that religion cannot make sense and that it must be just believed.

Islam teaches that Religion is the most important aspect of human life. It must be adopted consciously after careful thought, critique, evaluation and rationalization. It must make sense and appeal to our intellect. Even those born in Muslim families must re-evaluate, challenge and accept or reject their faith rationally. They must make a personal choice and consciously adopt Islam.

Although not all Muslims might have adopted Islam consciously in their life, a deliberate, well thought-out commitment is expected of them. If the human intellect is not honestly and sincerely sold on its truth, the belief in Islam is invalid. To be acceptable to God, both heart and mind must witness the truth of the faith. Thus it behoves every Muslim to give Islam an urgent attention and make it their personal, deliberate and conscious choice through appropriate rational and intellectual reasoning. Similarly every non-Muslim should critically review his or her beliefs in comparison with Islamic assertions and evaluate what makes the most sense. ✳

Chapter 2

A Rational Approach to
Questions About God

WHEN it comes to God, people have thought and fought about Him since time immemorial. But the issue remains unsettled. One reason is that the existence of God can neither be proven nor unproven conclusively. It does not matter which side one takes, there is no absolute proof for or against the existence of God. Because of the historical baggage of religious conflicts and impossibility of conclusive results, people do not even like to approach this subject. But the evasion of the issue is not going to change the reality. Nor is avoidance of the subject going to reduce the importance of everyone's need to consciously arrive at their own reality in their own rational manner to their own inner satisfaction.

You may be wondering: Is it possible to tackle this issue rationally to a reasonable degree of a person's own inner satisfaction? The answer is a very resounding yes, provided you open your mind and honestly reflect on the subject in an organized manner.

Usually, human beings learn about, discover or prove the reality of things in three ways: through sensory perceptions, through logical inferences and through reliance on the expert testimony of credible witnesses. Let us examine if these three tools can help in any meaningful way in the quest for God.

God and Our Sensory Perceptions

The basic technique we use to know about the material things that exist around us is to see, touch, hear, taste, smell, feel, observe or explore them through our senses, with or without the help of sophisticated instruments. A disciplined and controlled use of these methods provides us with scientific knowledge. We have amassed a vast amount of knowledge through these means. Society as a whole has been preserving what it learnt earlier and has been building upon that knowledge to advance its understanding of and discoveries in new fields. So far, we have been able to build a tremendous knowledge base so that many phenomena are well understood by humankind; some are being studied; and, still others will be explored and understood in the future.

The common characteristics of all things to which the above-mentioned scientific means can be applied is that they are all material things and they are all finite. From a simple situation to the most complex phenomena and from the huge galaxies to the invisible sub-atomic particles, everything is finite; i.e., it has a specific origin, life span, size, mass, charge, or form. Thus, the limitation of our scientific means or tools of knowledge is that their subject matter can only be finite, material things.

In addition, the human mind has its own limitations. Just like the scientific tools, our finite minds, too, can only perceive, relate to, visualize, understand, or imagine physical, finite objects. Even from the finite entities, we can only understand, visualize or imagine those entities that we have already learned or experienced personally. We are utterly incapable of imagining, understanding or visualizing something that we have never seen, perceived or experienced in any fashion. Just as a person who is born blind cannot imagine, understand or visualize colours, we cannot visualize what we have not seen; we cannot understand what we have not experienced; and we cannot imagine what we have not perceived in the past.

Because of these limitations, our sensory perceptions, scientific tools or mental faculties are of limited value in helping us arrive at some position about God, Who is neither finite, nor perceivable through any of our senses or tools.

A proper understanding of the capabilities of human faculties and the limitations of the mind is, however, extremely important in order to develop an appropriate outlook to life and to proceed further in exploring the reality of God. People's lifestyles and perceptions about God have been deeply impacted by the perspective they have had about the limitations and capabilities of our minds and the boundaries of human knowledge. As with anything else, there have been extreme as well as mixed views, each resulting in a different kind of human personality and a different kind of society.

On one extreme there are those who refuse to acknowledge the limitations of our minds, knowledge and understanding. To them, whatever is beyond our understanding or perception must not exist. They totally reject the idea of God because they cannot perceive, visualize or prove His existence. The fallacy of this attitude has been witnessed time and again by new scientific discoveries that prove the existence of things we never thought existed, thus refuting the earlier "ultimate" conclusions of "nothing exists beyond what we have proven." Neutrons, protons and electrons were the only particles believed to exist until neutrinos were discovered. There are many things we are not aware of, cannot think of, and cannot perceive or visualize, but they do exist. The colour of green grass, a red rose or white snow is still there even if a blind person cannot see or perceive it. For ages, human beings did not know of the existence of bacteria, but bacteria did not cease to exist or to infect. The same is true of viruses. An ordinary person cannot see, feel, touch, hear or smell a virus, but viruses do exist. Thus, for people to reject God because they cannot perceive Him or because they have not physically discovered Him is not rational.

On the other extreme there are those who are so inhibited and overpowered by the limitations of human capacity that anything and everything that seems more powerful or beyond their level of understanding becomes their object of worship. They are overawed by everything mysterious or better than them in any respect. Every such thing is given some kind of divine status. Idolaters fall in this category. Some of the people in this category cannot even relate to the idea of a non-physical, metaphysical or infinite entity beyond their imagination. They need to have a physical object as a deity to represent the powers of the things they do not understand or know about.

In between these two extremes are the people who recognize the appropriate limits of the mind and its faculties. Their logical approach is that anything that is finite cannot be worth worshipping. It might be worth exploring, looking into or researching for developing more understanding, but nothing beyond that. On the other hand, they do not deny God just because He is not perceivable or because things can be explained without bringing Him into the picture. Their minds are still open to God.

The fact that neither the existence of God nor His non-existence can be proven in material terms leaves two choices: the existence of God has to be inferred logically, established through the testimony of some credible witnesses, or both. Thus, if we can reach a stance that is logically the most reasonable, rationally sensible, consistent with our other observations in life and corroborated by the testimony of credible expert witnesses, we can adopt that stance and live by it with confidence and peace of mind.

Logical Inference

One point that is clearly and consistently demonstrated by our scientific research as well as by our common experiences is that every finite thing, without a single exception, is subject to the law of cause and effect. Everything that happens or ceases to happen does so because someone or something caused it. Throughout our life and throughout the existence of human beings, no one has ever seen anything happen without someone making it happen. Hence, we can safely infer that this magnificent universe was brought into existence by a "someone" we can call the Creator.

We have also seen that whenever we want anything meaningful or useful to happen, it has to be a well planned, methodological effort based on knowledge and wisdom. In the absence of knowledge, wisdom, plan, or methodology, nothing fruitful occurs and no improvements are possible. Accidents and random occurrences never produce fruitful results. That is why when we find some useful, meaningful work whose creator or the means of creation is not known to us, we never harbour the idea that it may have happened by chance or accident. We look at the Pyramids, but never assume that they came into being through some random occurrence of nature, though we have no conclusive evidence that the Pharaoh's people built them. We discover nice, big chambers carved in the mountains of Petra (the rock city), but no one has ever surmised that they must have come into being as a result of random geological accidents. The evidence of use of these amazing structures by human beings is not a proof of their being built by humans, just as the use of caves by primitive people does not mean that the cavemen built the caves. The only reason we believe that the Pyramids were built by Egyptians and the Petra chambers by Nabataeans is because historians claim so and because those structures could not have come into existence without the expertise of intelligent builders. In the same manner, we can deduce that as superb a creature as a human being must have been a planned creation of a wise, knowledgeable creator, as has been claimed by religious people.

Some people differentiate between human endeavours and work of natural forces. In doing so, they imply that this universe is run under multiple inconsistent laws, not a set of uniform laws applicable to all finite things. Perhaps they differentiate between the two because functioning of natural phenomena is not as explicit as human activity. They observe things like the vegetation life cycle or ecological balance continuing to maintain itself in a jungle and conclude that it is continuing automatically without anyone doing it. But does its continuation mean that it came into being on its own and it programmed itself to continue in that way, while the right soil conditions and the right weather in terms of appropriate amount of water, temperature and sunlight coincidentally happened to be available? The example is like my porch light that has sensors built in. It comes on when it is dark or when there is some motion detected, and it goes off when the day is bright; or, like a fully automated plant where the environmental and mechanical controls turn on and off automatically according to the conditions within the plant and the status of production cycle. Will it be right for someone visiting from Amazon jungle to conclude that my porch light or the automated factory came into being and is running on its own without some knowledgeable person designing, planning and producing it, and that electricity that powers it just coincidentally happened to be there for it to use? This is parallel to an atheist who thinks a tree took its present shape and programmed its development and reproduction on its own without knowledge, wisdom or planning on the Creator's part for its creation, its reproduction or the provision of the right weather and rainfall.

Those who assume it developed and programmed itself on its own to function in that manner are making a huge assumption, wild guess, superstitious conjecture, that lacks any support from Human experience. Whatever evidence is presented in support of this assumption is always more guesswork and assumption built upon previous conjectures. Every discovery that is claimed to be evidence has, at best, only been indicative of an evolutionary process, never indicative of something happening on its own without someone making it happen according to His knowledge, wisdom and power.

The reality is that whatever human beings say about creation is going to be conjecture, guess or unsupported theory. If a Creator created everything, then the only reliable means of information can be what He Himself tells us about it[1]. If creation was an accident of nature, the only evidence that will be acceptable in this regard is that we discover, observe and document another brand new creation while it is taking place through random occurrences. Until denied by the Creator or refuted by a new accidental creation, the logical stance is to rely on consistent human observation that every finite entity comes into being because someone makes it happen.

While every finite entity does have a creator, the Ultimate Creator (the Cause of causes) could not have been created by anyone and thus, by definition, has to be infinite — having no beginning, end, or limit

---

[1] This subject will be covered under the next heading; here we just want to restrict the discussion to logical interference.

of any kind whatsoever. Similarly, the Infinite Creator can be one and only one. There cannot be another infinite being. He has to be unique, as only finite entities can be more than one. Thus, He cannot have a spouse or child, nor can He have a gender[2]. He cannot be divisible into different personalities, as only finite entities can be divided. By the same token, He cannot be partitioned into different roles because partitioning means putting limits that negate infiniteness. He cannot have a certain image or shape that we can perceive or understand because we can perceive or understand only finite entities. He has to be omnipresent and not stationed or restricted to a location because finite locations cannot contain Infinity. By the same token, finite beings cannot claim incarnation of Infinity. He must be living at all times, without any iterruption in His existence and without any lapse in taking care of His creations. Similarly, He must not require food, rest or sleep. In short, He cannot have an imperfection, weakness or finite limit of any kind. This Infinite Creator is our God. He is infinite in person, existence, and all attributes like knowledge, wisdom, and power.

His infinity is precisely the reason for His being beyond our perception. We human beings can perceive and understand only the things we have experienced in life. If we have never experienced (seen, observed, heard, smelled, touched) something, no one can make us fully understand it. Just imagine if you have to explain colour to a person who was born blind. How would you explain yellow, green or red to such a person? When it comes to God, we are like a person blind from birth trying to understand colour. We have never experienced or perceived infinity and it is beyond our capacity to do so. Hence, we cannot fully understand it.

---

[2] The use of the male pronoun for Him does not mean to imply that Allaah has gender. Considering that our languages do not have a special pronoun for the Infinite Creator, we automatically defer to the masculine singular form of the pronoun.

Not being able to understand the infinite creator means that we cannot describe Him through our own ideas, imagination or feelings. We cannot speculate on our own about His attributes. We can say about Him only what He himself tells us through extremely reliable and undoubtedly trustworthy sources.

Logically, then, the most reasonable and sensible idea is to believe in a Creator (God) Who is Infinite, thus, One and Unique. But is there any testimonial evidence to support this rational, logical conclusion? Certainly there is! In fact, this logical approach is only the first step towards recognizing God, the Creator of the universe. The majority of humanity subscribes to this idea on the strength of expert witness consistently given by a series of extraordinary people throughout human history.

Expert Witness

In our day-to-day life, we not only accept the things we have personally perceived, observed, watched, discovered, explored, or experienced, but we also believe in many things that people we trust tell us about.

A blind person walking on the road believes in his companion for the presence of traffic lights and relies on him to know the green light from the red.

Most of us have never seen evidence of the existence of viruses but we believe in the experts' claims about them. A doctor tells a sick person that her disease is caused by a virus: the sick person believes the doctor without ever having a chance of seeing the virus itself, without knowing exactly what a virus looks like and without understanding how it causes the sickness. We believe in the doctor because we have confidence that the doctor knows the reality of that sickness and that he is giving an honest opinion on the basis of his knowledge. In fact, at that time, neither the doctor nor the patient is able to observe the presence of the virus. They rely on the pronouncements of experts and the symptoms caused by the virus.

Thus, to know about something or to believe in its existence, we do not have to observe the evidence of its existence personally. Often we rely on witnesses of the experts in various fields.

All the knowledge we have been able to accumulate was only possible because every human being did not re-invent the wheel by starting from the beginning, but relied on the experience and expert witness of the teachers who had previously acquired certain knowledge. Especially we, the common people, rely for many things on scientists and we take as truth what they tell us. The more the scientists express the same opinion, the more we believe in their version of the reality of their subject matter. Also, the more consistent they are, the more confidence we have in our belief of their statements. For example, we are told about the existence of neutrinos and quarks. Both my teacher and I have never observed their existence, but we rely on the integrity of researchers and the papers they have written on the topic.

Our belief in things mentioned to us by other people depends on the confidence and trust we have in their honesty, knowledge and expertise. In other words, our faith in people is relative to the credibility they have in our minds.

Throughout human history, there have been people who had much credibility with their society in terms of their honesty, truthfulness, wisdom, and intelligence. They were always the best, most highly regarded and most respected people of their society. They lived very modest, but pure and highly moral lives. None of them had any personal axe to grind or selfish motive to satisfy. On the other hand, they made immense sacrifices and lived selfless lives. Although they were raised at different times in different nations speaking different languages, they all said the same thing. They made the same claims and promoted exactly the same philosophy. Unlike the modern scientist we put much faith in, they were extremely consistent in their claim, message and proposition. They were people like Noah, Abraham, Isaac, Moses, Jesus and Muhammad, peace be upon all of them. Over time, there have been thousands of them. They all told us of the existence of One God and they told us clearly that they are not just assuming it logically, rather, they have personal knowledge of His existence and that they have constant communication with Him. Their lives were consistent with their statements, indicating that they were true to their claims. The depth of their knowledge, the excellence of their practice and the quality of their discourses proved that they were experts in their field. They even identified the signs of God in our own being, in the creations of God surrounding us, in the universe, and in the systems of nature sustaining the life on our planet. For the job of giving us the news about God and for bringing us His message, they were called prophets and messengers[3].

Their credibility was further sustained by the fact that anyone who believed in them tasted sweetness of their faith through a genuine relationship with their Creator so much so that no amount of persecution and tyranny could ever make them lose faith or decrease their trust in and respect for those witnesses.

A question may be asked as to how these people were able to know God, the Infinite, when no other human being can. The interesting thing to remember is that none of these knowledgeable witnesses had volunteered himself for, or was desirous of, taking this responsibility. It is God Who selected these outstanding individuals and gave them the special knowledge in finite terms that they could handle and relate to.

[3] For more details, see 'Rational Vindication of Prophethood and Hereafter' by Syed Abul A'la Maudoodi

A question may also be raised about the consistency of their message, as there appear to be many inconsistencies about the concept of God contained in religious books. This problem is caused by two factors: describing an "infinite" being in finite terms, and the limitations of the writers who carry the message to subsequent generations.

1. If someone tries to describe or explain to us something that we have never experienced, it has to be through the things we already know. I once had to describe the taste of mango to some colleagues who had never tasted one. It was difficult. The best I could do was to compare it with the tastes of the fruits they had tasted. That is our limitation. Unfamiliar concepts can only be described or explained in terms of the concepts we are familiar with. Hence God, although Infinite, is described to us in the finite terms we can relate to. We can learn about Him only through the attributes we are familiar with, though they take infinite meanings when describing Him.

2. When subsequent generations put these messages in their own words, the message is miscoded. The miscoding is caused by the incapacity of the writers to comprehend the infinite concepts properly and by the limitations of the human language to describe infinite concepts. The miscoded message is interpreted by the readers in their own way according to their own crude understanding of God and is generally misunderstood because of the inability of readers to transcend the crudeness of those finite words. Gradually the message gets distorted sometimes to the extent that God is described in very inappropriate finite terms. (Examples of such distortions will be provided in later sections.) Despite all these difficulties and apparent inconsistencies, if we honestly look behind the words, the message about the existence of an Infinite Creator comes out consistently loud and clear. In the case of Islam, however, the original message has been preserved in original words so faithfully that the pure, pristine message is always available to anyone who wants to explore the truth[4].

---

[4] For details, please refer to the author's articles on the Qur'aan

What *is* His Name?

THIS Infinite Creator is called Allaah in Islam. He is the same God who was worshipped by all prophets and messengers like Adam, Noah, Abraham, Moses, David, John, Jesus and Muhammad. Although God, the Creator, can be called by any name, we do not prefer to use the word God because it is not befitting the infinity and uniqueness of the Creator for reasons such as the following:

- *When speaking, God (the true God) cannot be distinguished from god (a false god).*
- *It sounds as if the "God" is a special one out of a species of gods, just like the man is one particular person from all men. It is also subject to plurality (gods).*
- *It is subject to gender (goddess), begging the question why call Him God, not Goddess; and,*
- *To different people, God means different things. Over time, many misconceptions and mythology have come to be attributed to and attached with the word God.*

We prefer to call Him Allaah for the following reasons:

- *It is the personal name God has chosen for Himself [5];*
- *It has never been used for a false god;*
- *It is not subject to plurality or gender. Thus it is a fitting, unique name for the infinite, one and unique Creator;*
- *There are no mythological misconceptions attached with it; and,*
- *Previous messengers like Abraham, Jesus and Moses also called Him Allaah.*

Footnotes for this page are located on the last page of this chapter.

The Rational Conclusion

As we can see, the logical inference about the existence of the Infinite God is corroborated by the signs of nature and validated by the consistent testimony of the noble experts who witnessed on the basis of their personal knowledge, not conjecture. Hence, it makes good sense to believe that:

- *There is a Creator who is One, Unique, Infinite and Absolute;*
- *We cannot specify His image or shape;*
- *There is no one like Him or equal to Him;*
- *He does not have beginning or end, nor parents or child; and,*
- *The human body cannot contain him through incarnation or any other way.*

---

5 God told Moses, "Indeed I am Allaah; there is no God besides me..." The Qur'aan 20:14

He told Muhammad, "Say! He is Allaah, the One and the Unique." The Qur'aan 112:1

In Hebrew 'Elohim' a plural form of respect for 'Alah', used along with Yahuwah (Jehovah) about 6000 times in the Hebrew manuscripts of the Old testament, but translated as God. For details see "What is His Name" by Ahmed Deedat

In the New Testament, the person on the cross shouted, "Elohi, Elohi, ..." or "Eli, Eli ...", My Allaah! My Allaah! (Mark 15:34 and Matthew 27:46)

Chapter 3

How Were We Created?

ALTHOUGH it is very reasonable to believe that we are the creation of a creator, some people are reluctant to adopt this point of view because of the very unscientific way the act of creation has been described in some religious books. Some books describe it as if God, like a human being, needs to do things with His own hands. He shaped dust into human form and then blew air into it to make it alive. Obviously, this is not only unscientific but also against the majesty of the Infinite God. Allaah does not work through the finite means we are accustomed to but through infinite ways beyond our imagination.

Islamic Version of Reality

Islam contends categorically and forcefully that this universe has been created by Allaah. He is the Creator of this universe and everything in it. To make this point, the Qur'aan (Islamic scripture) gives examples of the evidence that indicates the existence, control and authority of Allaah — the evidence that is readily available in human nature itself, in the ecosystems within which we subsist, and in this magnificent universe that surrounds us[6]. This evidence is presented so that the thinkers, the learned, the wise, and those who have common sense can positively perceive the existence, understand the need and feel the presence of Allaah.

Islam, however, does not describe the process of creation.Obviously God's infinite ways are indescribable in finite human language. The Qur'aan gives some pointers towards the process in terms of the concepts that can be meaningful to people of any society at any time. The gist of those pointers can be described in the following paragraphs.

From the Islamic point of view, Allaah possesses absolute power, infinite wisdom and eternal knowledge. Because of these ultimate powers, He does not have to resort to actively doing something manually. Whatever He wills just happens as and when He wants. He commands it to be and it occurs[7]. He brought the universe into being with His command and the process of its formation started taking place with a big bang that scattered and shaped the matter in the form of galaxies, stars and planets[6]. His command

---

[6] There are numerous verses in the Holy Qur-aan that invite people's attention to the Signs of Allaah. For example:

"And a sign for them is the dead land. We gave it life and produced grain from it, which they eat. And we developed therein orchards of date-palms and grapes, and caused therein springs to gush forth, so that they eat its fruit. It was not their hands that made all this. Will they not thank? Glorified is He Who has created pairs (male/female) of every thing, whether it is earth's produce or the people themselves or the things they do not know about. And a sign for them is the night: We remove the day from it and they are plunged in darkness. And the sun: it runs its course for a fixed term as per the decree of the All-Mighty, All-Knowing. And the Moon: We have predestined stages for it till it reverts to a shape like a shrivelled date-stalk. Neither is it possible for the sun to overtake the moon, nor for the night to outpace the day. Each floats in its own orbit. The Qur'aan 36:33-40

Another example is chapter Ar-Room (Rome) where a series of signs of Allaah have been mentioned eloquently. The Qur'aan 30:20-27

[7] "When He intends something, He says to it, 'Be!' so it happens." The Qur'aan 36:82

"To Allaah, Jesus is like Adam whom He created from dust. He said to him, 'Be!' So he was." The Qur'aan 3:59

[8] "Have the disbelievers not considered that the heavens and earth were a joined entity (compacted mass) and we separated them, and with water We gave life to every living thing. Then will they not believe?" The Qur'aan 21:30

determined the universal laws of nature according to which the formation was going to progress and according to which the universe was going to operate for as long as He wanted it to operate on those laws. Because of Allaah's absolute power, perfect knowledge and ultimate wisdom, His decreed laws were such which would automatically keep functioning and producing the results He wanted to produce during the development of the universe and forever thereafter. Those laws were going to work consistently throughout the planned life of this universe. What we call the laws of nature are actually the laws that Allaah decreed for the creation and operation of the universe. We have discovered many of these laws of nature through our scientific research, we may discover some more in the future, and some we may never be able to figure out.

Because the laws of nature are the laws decreed by Allaah to fulfill His own plans, anything that results from the operation of these laws can justifiably be regarded as Allaah's work.

The developmental process of the universe continued until things took the shape Allaah wanted them to take and it will continue until the universe destroys itself at the end of its life, which has been predetermined in Allaah's plan. To reach maturity, the universe went through six stages[9]. Each stage may have taken hundreds of thousands, millions or billions of years in terms of time, as we know

---

[9] "And it is He Who created the heavens and earth in six periods, while His throne was on water, so that He may test who of you performs the best." The Qur'aan 11:7

"And indeed We created the heavens and the earth and everything between them in six periods, and We were not fatigued." The Qur'aan 50:38

it. That knowledge has not been shared with us by Allaah perhaps because the time each stage took is beyond our comprehension. Or, perhaps because our concept of defining and measuring time is relative only to the earth and its solar system, and is, therefore not suitable to measure time before the earth took its present shape. Scientists have tried to guess the age of the universe, and with every discovery of new knowledge, the figure is revised. It does not matter how much we know, without the benefit of definite knowledge from the Creator, it will always be an educated guess and nothing more. In any case, the specifics of time are irrelevant for the purposes of knowing our Creator or our relationship with Him.

Allaah also created angels to carry out certain duties in addition to natural laws to fulfill His plans. In keeping with Allaah's plans, life appeared wherever He wanted in His universe. One such place was the earth, where, as Allaah willed and commanded, different life forms came into being through the work of His angels and His laws of nature.

So far, no creation was granted free will or the freedom to make choices. They were all bound by laws of nature or pre-programmed through their instincts. Then came the Jinn[10], the first creation to have the freedom to make choices[11].

---

[10] Jinns are a creation of Allaah that are normally invisible to human beings, but are distinct from angels: "And Jinns We had created them before (Adam) from the smokeless flame of fire." The Qur'aan 15:27

[11] Jinns are quoted saying, "There are among us some who are righteous and some the contrary; we are groups having different ways." The Qur'aan 72:11

Also, "And indeed the Jinns know well that they certainly will be presented (for Judgment)." The Qur'aan 37:158

At the opportune stage of the maturity of the universe, somewhere in the universe beyond the earth[12], Allaah's laws of nature worked according to His Will and Plan to start the creation of human beings. Human beings were not only to have freedom to make decisions and choices about their behaviour and lifestyle, but also a quest to discover, know and learn. From the moment of Allaah's Will to create human beings until His laws of nature worked to produce human beings, there was a process of creation which, by its very nature, was evolutionary. As mentioned earlier, the exact nature of the evolutionary process or its details as to where it took place, the time it took and the stages it went through is knowledge that Allaah has not shared with us. The only information we have been given is that the starting point of the process was an essence (or extract) from sticky, rotten mud, like potter's clay. After initial creation, there was a proportioning or improvement process, at the completion of which the spirit was bestowed[13].

---

[12] "And We said, 'O Adam! You and your wife live in the Gardens (heavens).'" The Qur'aan 2:35

---

[13] "He began the creation of man from clay." The Qur'aan 32:7

"And indeed We created man from an essence (extract) of clay." The Qur'aan 23:12

"Verily, We created them of sticky clay." The Qur'aan 37:11

"He created man from sounding clay like the clay of pottery." The Qur'aan 55:14

"And when your Lord said to the angels: 'I am going to create a human being from sounding clay of rotten mud. So when I have proportioned him to perfection and infused into him the soul I created, then fall down prostrating yourselves unto him." The Qur'aan 15:28-29

Exactly as Allaah planned and willed, the process produced a couple[14] (a male and a female) of perfect human beings who had all the proper shape, psyche, instincts, features, potentials, weaknesses, and qualities that present day human beings have. This couple was brought to the earth to live and procreate here for a predetermined period of time[15]. Because this new creation, the human beings, had freedom to make decisions and was given some knowledge on which to base these decisions, it was bestowed with a limited amount of supremacy and authority (dominion) over its surroundings so that it could implement its decisions and choices[16].

---

[14] "O people! Certainly, We created you from a male and a female and made you clans and tribes only to enable you to recognize one another." The Qur'aan 49:13

"O people! Be dutiful to your Lord Who has created you from a single soul, and of the same He created his mate and from them both He spread countless men and women." The Qur'aan 4:1

---

[15] "We decreed, 'Go down you all as enemies to one another. Your stay and livelihood will be on earth for a specified time.'" The Qur'aan 2:36 'Specified time' for individuals is the human life span and for the humanity as a whole, it is the time fixed for the end of the world.

---

[16] "And when Your Lord said to Angels, 'I am going to appoint a vicegerent on the earth'." The Qur'aan 2:30

"We presented the trust (freedom of choice along with the delegation of authority and consequent accountability) to the heavens and the earth and the mountains, but they declined to bear it and were afraid of it, while the man undertook it." The Qur'aan 33:73

Although we are curious and want to know more details of Allaah's creative processes, we really do not need to know the age of the universe or the process of our creation in order to make scientific progress, to advance in technology, to function properly, or to live a good life. Perhaps for that reason, for human incapacity to comprehend and for all other reasons that we do not know, Allaah in His ultimate wisdom did not share this knowledge with us. Whatever knowledge we need for our progress is available in finite forms for us to discover through our scientific research. Extremely important, however, is to know that we are His creation.

To help us in knowing Him and believing in Him without seeing or perceiving Him, Allaah has taken special measures such as the following:

1. First of all, He coded into the human psyche a need to accept Allaah as the Creator. That is why the overwhelming majority of people always have some concept of a God in whom they believe. Those who do not believe in Him find a certain feeling of spiritual emptiness regardless of how wealthy or accomplished they are. To fill the spiritual void created by the quest for God, people may resort to overindulgence in the pleasures of the world, but they do not fill the void. Its fulfillment remains a mirage until Allaah is believed in.

2. Human beings cross the line of childhood into adulthood when they come of age and physical changes happen to their bodies. For this stage in people's lives, Allaah has put into the human instinct an urge to challenge the accepted beliefs and norms of society so that every person can free himself from the ideas indoctrinated

into their minds by society and everyone can freely choose his own beliefs. It is only after this stage in a person's life that Allaah has made human beings responsible for their actions.

3. When people reach mid-life, Allaah gives them another chance to re-evaluate the life they have been living. An emotional upheaval, which nudges us to reconsider our life, gives us another chance to come back to Allaah. Also, at the difficult moments of our lives, when we realize our powerlessness, we feel the need and presence of Allaah and we come back to recognize Him.

4. He chose special human beings at various times and places among various communities of people all over the globe and educated them about Himself. He then made them responsible to teach their communities about Him. As has previously been mentioned, they are people like Noah, Abraham, Moses, Jesus, and Muhammad, peace be upon all of them.

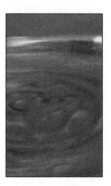

Chapter 4

Why Were We Created?

✹

JUST as we know from our experience that everything in this universe has been created, we also know that everything that exists has a purpose, role or objective to fulfill. Everything we know of in our life has a purpose for which it is created and used. Even every part, limb, organ or cell of our body has a purpose. It all indicates that human beings themselves must have a purpose as well. In addition, if we are a planned creation of a wise and knowledgeable Creator, as has been shown previously, it only makes sense that He must have created us for a purpose. Our creation must mean something more than just eat, drink and die. Our life must have a more profound and more significant purpose than living, dying and leaving everything behind. The question arises: What is that purpose? Why did Allaah create us?

Every creation of Allaah, except for Jinns[17] and human beings, obeys the laws and commands of Allaah and performs as it is destined to perform[18]. Thus all those creations are fully obedient to Allaah.

---

[17] Conscious beings that are invisible to us, were created before us, and enjoy freedom of action like us.

---

[18] "So do they seek other than the Allaah's Deen (religion and way of life), while to Him have submitted everything in the heavens and the earth (the whole universe), willingly or unwillingly?..." The Qur'aan 3:83

It is only because of the continuous, consistent obedience of all the creations to Allaah that the universe is functioning well and is in balance and equilibrium. Had that not been the case, there would have been chaos and destruction. The universe would not last or sustain itself and life would be impossible. None of these creations, however, have any choice but to follow the laws of Allaah. They do not have freedom to behave differently. Their purpose is defined and so is their fate to fulfill that purpose. Thus, their obedience is predestined, not chosen.

Allaah gave human beings and Jinns freedom to choose. Although in terms of their physical being they are subject to the laws of nature in the same way as animals or plants are, in terms of their behaviour and lifestyles they are left to make their own decisions and their own choices.

The purpose of human creation was, as Allaah Himself has told us through his prophets and messengers, to have a creature that would worship and obey Him[19] of its own accord and by its own choice,[20] without being predestined or forced to obey through the laws of nature and instincts, like other creatures have been. People were to be given an eternal life, except that there was a quirk.

---

[19] "I did not create Jinn and humans except for the purpose that they serve Me like slaves." The Qur'aan 51:56

---

[20] "We created man from a drop of mixed semen and, to test him, made him hearer and seer. Verily, We have showed him the way, whether he be grateful or ungrateful." The Qur'aan 76:2-3

If all humanity would follow Allaah's commands in total servitude (worship) to Allaah, their actions would be moderate, balanced, fair and equitable, just like the rest of the universe. In that case, human society would be a peaceful and content society in harmony with its environment and nature. The environment on the planet Earth would remain in equilibrium and the whole universe, the Kingdom of Allaah, would continue to function perfectly as designed by Allaah. Obviously, with freedom of choice being available, not all human beings would follow the lifestyle decreed by Allaah. The actions of the disobedient people would thus be unbalanced, excessive, extreme, and exploitive. If a majority of human beings disobeyed Allaah's commands, human excesses would result in the disaster of natural environment and the lack of peace, harmony and fairness in human society.

If Allaah were to give permanence to human beings just as they were, the disobedient people would create problems and chaos in His universe by their bad behaviour. Allaah would not want the order and peace of His universal kingdom disturbed by the disobedient people forever. Hence, Allaah decided to put human beings first in a temporary world so that each human being could be tested for his or her preference for the path of obedience or that of disobedience. A system of birth, growth and death was put in place so that each person had an opportunity to prove whether he or she could responsibly handle the authority afforded by free choice or resorted to disobedience when given freedom. People would be born for a temporary stay on this earth as a test period. This would continue until the Day of Judgment when the existing solar system along with all its inhabitants would be destroyed and re-created with new natural laws[21]. On that day, the people — every single one of them since inception — would be brought back to life and segregated according to their lifestyle of obedience or disobedience. From that day onwards, an eternal life would start where only the obedient people would have total freedom in the Gardens of Paradise. There, they would have a very rewarding and luxurious life. The people who abused their God-given freedom by choosing the path of disobedience in this life will be imprisoned and punished in Hell. The abusers of their freedom having been put away, there would be eternal peace and order in the whole universal kingdom of Allaah, including the newly re-created earth.

It is according to this plan and for this purpose that Allaah created us and put us on the earth[22]. That being the case, we must obey and worship Allaah by our own choice as fully and wholly as every other creation is programmed to do. To those who do not do so, Allaah says:

> *Have you assumed that we have created you without any*
> *purpose and that you would not be brought back to Us?*
> *In fact, Allaah, the real Sovereign, is far too Exalted*
> *(to do anything purposeless). There is no God But He,*
> *the Lord of the Throne of Grace.*
>
> — *The Qur'aan 23:115-116*

---

[21] "The day when the earth will be replaced with another earth and the heavens as well, and people will come out before Allaah, the One, the Prevailing." The Qur'aan 14:48

---

[22] "We presented the trust (freedom of choice along with the delegation of authority and consequent accountability) to the heavens and the earth and the mountains, but they declined to bear it and were afraid of it, while the man undertook it. Indeed, he was unjust (to himself), ignorant (of the implications). The objective being that Allaah punishes the hypocrites and the Mushriks (those who do not serve Allaah solely and purely) and accepts the repentance of the believers. Allaah is really the Most-Forgiving, the Most-Merciful." The Qur'aan 33:73

Those who reflect sincerely on the creation and operation of the universe and our solar system come to the foregoing conclusion. Their mental state is portrayed in the following verses of the Holy Qur'aan:

Verily, in the creation of the heavens and the earth, and in the alternation of night and day, there are definite signs for sensible, understanding persons – those who always think about Allaah while standing, sitting or lying on their sides, and who ponder over creation and operation of the universe. (They exclaim):

"Our Lord! You have not created all this in vain. Your Glory is above and beyond (indulging in purposeless acts). So, save us from the torment of the Fire. Our Lord! Whomever you cast into the Fire will indeed be disgraced and never will such transgressors find any helpers. Our Lord! We heard a caller calling to the Faith, saying: 'Believe in your Lord.' So we believed. Hence, Our Lord! Forgive us our sins and remit our evil deeds from us and let our end be with the righteous people."

– The Qur'aan 3: 190-193

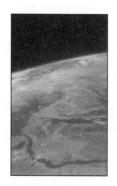

Chapter 5

The Forgiveness and Mercy of Allaah

THE previous chapter indicated that we have been placed on the earth for a temporary test at the end of which we will be judged, and then rewarded or punished according to our performance in the test. To some people these statements seem to pose a problem: We human beings are not perfect; even the most excellent of human beings sometimes slips and sins; so how can anyone, then, succeed in the test of obedience to Allaah?

The answer is simple. Although Allaah has created us to be fully obedient to him throughout our lives, He does not expect us to be perfect because perfection is beyond human capacity. Allaah does not require of us anything that is beyond our capacity. Even those who try their best to remain obedient to Allaah may sometimes get into a random instance of undesirable behaviour because of an oversight, a lapse in determination or a lowering of their guard.

What is expected of us is to stay on the course of obedience, not to be perfect in obedience. When we slip off and sin, we should immediately repent and seek Allaah's forgiveness. For those who are generally obedient and for whom an act of disobedience is out of line with their character, He is very forgiving and merciful[23].

---

[23] "And Indeed, I am very forgiving to whoever repents, believes and performs good deeds, and then continues in guidance." The Qur'aan 20:82

He forgives them as soon as they are truly remorseful and ask Him sincerely for forgiveness. However, there has to be a genuine remorse, sincere repentance and unfaltering determination to remain fully obedient to Him. If these qualities are present, Allaah promises forgiveness out of His Mercy. Nobody has to die to attain forgiveness for people except their own evil desires. A genuine struggle to remain obedient is all that is required by our Forgiving and Merciful Creator. By reason of His boundless Mercy,[24] He forgives the sincere repenters as soon as they repent.

The beauty of Allaah's mercy is that once a person is forgiven, his slate is wiped clean. Our sincere repentance deletes the old records of our sins. They do not reappear. Also, the repentance is a very direct and personal matter between each of us and our Creator. No intermediary or helper can help in this regard or come in between our relationship with our Creator. Everyone has to seek it directly from Allaah Who is well aware of how sincere we are in our repentance and our request for forgiveness.

His Mercy is indeed boundless. Irrespective of one's past, if at any time in one's life a person sincerely chooses to obey Allaah like a slave, Allaah forgives and accepts the person as such. Changing his lifestyle from disobedience to obedience becomes the expiation for all of his past sins.

---

[24] Tell (them), "O my slaves who have transgressed against themselves (by disobeying Me), do not despair of the mercy of Allaah. Verily, Allaah forgives all sins. Indeed, He is the Forgiving, the Merciful." The Qur'aan 39:53

The good news is that He has an open-door policy. The door remains open throughout our temporary sojourn on earth. As soon as we start handling our freedom of choice responsibly and deliberately choose to be His obedient servants, we qualify for freedom in the Hereafter. All we need to do is demonstrate that we are capable of being obedient of our own free will and that we can maintain the law and order in His universe the way He wants. We may have learnt to be that way through making many mistakes. We may have taken a long time to acquire that capability. The moment we become obedient by choice, His mercy prevails over us. If we continue to be in the state of voluntary obedience till our death, we are bestowed the freedom in the bliss of the Hereafter.

Another aspect of His Mercy is that sin is neither transferable nor inheritable. No one has to, nor can anyone bear the burden of another person's sins. A son does not inherit the sins of his father. Parents do not have to account for the sins of their adult offspring. Everyone is on his or her own. No one can bear the burden of another, nor can anyone cause the forgiveness for another[25]. Everyone has to attain forgiveness for himself or herself and everyone has to build their own credit balance with Allaah by doing good deeds. There is no original sin that we have to worry about. We are accounable only for the disobedience of our adult life (life since physical maturity and coming of age). Each one of us is the master of his or her own destiny.

---

[25] "That no bearer of burdens will bear the burden of another, and that there will be nothing for man except that for which he strives." The Qur'aan 53:38-39

Chapter 6

Problems In Perspective

BESTOWING freedom of choice upon human beings and giving them the authority to execute their decisions has two built-in dangers. Firstly, people can make wrong decisions because of the imperfection of human knowledge and wisdom. Secondly, people can choose to misuse their authority and disobey Allaah by practising injustice, violating rights or doing other improper acts. Both result in problems in society and loss of peace, justice and harmony. The likelihood of such occurrences increases significantly because people cannot perceive Allaah. It creates uncertainty about Him and makes people more prone to disobeying Him.

All of the injustices, exploitations, crimes, wars, environmental destruction, pollution, concentration of wealth in fewer hands vis-à-vis starvation of masses of people, etc. are examples of the problems created by the excesses committed by people in disobedience of the Creator. It is to weed out such people who misuse their freedom bestowed by Allaah and commit excesses that Allaah SWT put us in a temporary universe.

Making this world temporary also required building into it some imperfections. The natural laws had to be such that would lead to its own destruction. While it had to be made sustainable for a long period to let all planned generations of human beings find the earth hospitable and inhabitable, it must not have been perfect in all respects to continue in an ideal way forever. Some of its imperfections show up in the form of natural disasters. Natural disasters demonstrate to people the temporary nature of this world. They are a part of Allaah's plan as a sign of Allaah's power and authority. They remind people of the limits of the power and authority given to them in this world and the limitless power and authority of the Creator Himself. They put those who misuse their freedom in place and in check. Without such countermeasures and signs, the disobedient to Allaah would feel in full control of the affairs of the world and would rebel beyond limits creating insurmountable problems for other human beings.

Testing people through a temporary life had its own needs. Such natural laws for human life had to be ordained that would make the timing of a person's death unpredictable. An individual's span of life without a predictable time frame was designed so that people would prepare for death knowing that it can come anytime and that delaying obedience to God to a future time would be extremely risky because a future opportunity to repent and become obedient might not come. This required that people would die at different ages: some at very young age, some at very old age and others anywhere in between; and that such occurrence should appear random to people.

Those who do not understand these aspects of Allaah's plan tend to deny Allaah's existence on that basis. They think that if a Merciful Creator existed, He would not allow any injustice or crimes in the world. They do not realize that it is because of His mercy that He has put this temporary system in place to weed out the transgressors so that all others can have peace afterwards forever. They forget that once this short test is over, the victims of human crimes will enjoy the mercy of Allaah on the Day of Judgment and in the eternal life Hereafter. Similarly, some people question that if an omnipotent God were taking care of the universe, why would human beings suffer from natural disasters? They miss the point that these natural occurrences evidence the power of God, become signs for the rebellious, and remind the faithful of the need to prepare for the ultimate destruction on the Day of Judgement. They wonder why a kind God would let the innocent people or a child die. They forget that there is nothing cruel or unjust in moving people naturally to the next stage of life where it will be perfect in every respect, continue forever, discomfort-free and full of pleasures and joys for the obedient people. That is where we will experience the full limitlessness of the mercy of Allaah. Even those who bear the grief of these deaths in this world will be compensated generously in the hereafter for all the troubles they had to suffer. We are going through a temporary phase on a path towards an eternal bliss.

Some people may question: If Allaah has created us so that we obey and serve Him like slaves and create a society of peace and justice, why has He not pre-programmed us to do so as He has done to the angels and His other creations? And why did He not make Himself manifest to us and give us capability to know His existence beyond doubt? Why not make this life permanent with eternal bliss without putting us through this temporary test where people have opportunities to do bad things and others have to suffer?

The answers to these questions can become self-evident with a bit of reflection and pondering.

Making this life permanent and problem free would have required Him to pre-program our behaviour without giving us freedom to make decisions. If He were going to pre-program us for obedience, then there would be no need to create us because there were two groups of living creations already pre-programmed for obedience: animals as carnal creatures, and angels as spiritual beings who do not have any carnal needs. The only key difference between animals and humans is intellect and its use to acquire knowledge and to choose some behaviour other than that dictated by instincts. Pre-programmed human beings with carnal needs would not require intellect because no decision-making would be needed. They would be just another species of animals. Human beings without carnal needs would be like angels, who are already fulfilling that role perfectly. In either case, our creation would be redundant, purposeless and unnecessary, and it is far from the Glory and Majesty of Allaah to do something that is unnecessary and purposeless.

The other aspect is that any pre-programmed creation, such as an angel or an animal, can do only what is right and just. A creation that has freedom of choice, on the other hand, has the capacity to do more than what is right. It can do more than what is required; give more than what is due; respond with what is the best; and forgive, overlook and forget the wrongs of others. It can opt for excellence, compassion, mercy, magnanimity, generosity, and forgiveness. In this way, the creation that has free choice can reflect some of the qualities of the Creator in its behaviour, which a pre-programmed creature cannot. It is only in this sense that human beings have been created in the "image" of God.

By putting us temporarily on this earth, Allaah has given us the opportunity to show who of us is capable of portraying Allaah's qualities that go beyond justice— doing better than what is fair, expected or required. It is only these people who will enjoy freedom and bliss in the eternal life that is to come after this temporary life.

If Allaah had made Himself perceivable so that people knew His existence and presence with certainty, this life would be no test at all. The purpose of the test is to select human beings who can rise above the animal level, go beyond the carnal considerations, intellectually and spiritually perceive their Creator, grasp the metaphysical realities, and choose to obey that creator even if they have to forego some of their carnal urges in the course of that obedience. The perceivable presence of Allaah takes away the test element altogether. Who does not behave their best when the boss is right there watching? Who would not obey when the absolutely powerful and completely aware Master is watching right in front of everyone?

To identify the people with the right potential, Allaah has kept Himself hidden, though He is manifest through so many signs for the right kind of people to recognize Him. Those who want to see Him with certainty before believing in Him are behaving inconsistently with their normal modus operandi in life, as explained with examples previously[26], and are also exposing themselves to great dangers[27].

We make many decisions in our life without the benefit of definite knowledge to base our decisions upon. Lack of precise knowledge does not deter us from making those important decisions. We use our best judgment, take risks, and try to make a decision which makes the most sense, which will likely be the least risky, or which will most likely deliver the maximum benefit. We need to take the same approach in this extremely important matter of believing in Allaah.

---

[26] Examples were given to indicate that many decisions in life are made without certainty of knowledge.

---

[27] "Are they waiting but for Allaah to come to them in covers of clouds and angels (as well) and the matter is decided (the test is over and judgement takes place)?" The Qur'aan 2:210

"Are they waiting for anything except that angels come to them, or your Lord appears, or some of the signs of your Lord appear? The Day some of the signs of your Lord will appear, no soul will benefit from its faith if it had not believed before or had not earned some good through its faith." The Qur'aan 6:158

Chapter 7

What Does it All Mean to You Personally?

THE whole discussion so far can be summed up in the following points concerning the human relationship to Allaah:

- *This universe, everything in it and human beings have been created by One, Unique and Infinite Creator, Allaah;*

- *Allaah created us with freedom to make decisions regarding our behaviour, but with the purpose that we live in complete obedience to Him by our own free choice;*

- *Our stay in this world is temporary; everyone born must die;*

- *The life in this world is for the test of our obedience or disobedience;*

- *The world, as we know it, will end on the Day of Judgment. Any human beings still alive will also die on that day when the world is destroyed;*

- *Every human being will be raised from the dead again to live an eternal life; people will be segregated on the basis of the results of the obedience test of this life;*

- *The earth will be re-created under new physical laws; with bountiful, life-nourishing systems;*

- *The disobedient will be imprisoned and punished in Hell;*

- *The obedient servants of Allaah will enjoy freedom, comforts, pleasures and luxuries in a very rewarding, peaceful and eternal life in the Hereafter; and,*

- *Allaah does not expect perfection in obedience but a consistent effort to remain obedient. He accepts repentance and forgives out of His mercy when we slip in our efforts to remain obedient to Him.*

So far, the logic, common sense and testimony of the Messengers of Allaah all have indicated that it makes sense that there is a creator who has created us for a test and that we will be held accountable regarding our performance in the test. Those who accept this sensible conclusion and live by it will enjoy a huge payoff in the form of a luxurious life in the Hereafter. For argument's sake, if after death they find that not to be the case, the only risk they have taken is in giving up some of the instant pleasures their faith might have caused them to avoid. It is like a student going to university with the expectation of a well-paying career after graduation. The student sacrifices some of the pleasures while concentrating on studies, but the risk is there that the student might not find a dream job even after finishing university. In the case of Islam, even that is not much of a risk, because the true Islamic religious teachings are good for us even in this world. Hence for a paltry risk, the expected benefits are colossal.

On the other hand, those who disbelieve can live the way they like in this world without having to abide by any religious rules or regulations – a paltry gain, but they are taking a gigantic risk to suffer God's punishment in their life Hereafter. Considering the logic and reasoning presented so far, the possibility of this risk becoming a reality is much much more likely than the chance of there being no God or Hereafter.

Therefore, whether one wants to minimize the risk or maximize the rewards or both, the wise choice is to believe in Allaah and to obey Him in this life in preparation for accountability to Him in the Hereafter.

Some people, agnostics, prefer to stay undecided about this issue. Because neither the existence of God nor His non-existence can be proven beyond doubt, they think that it is logical to be agnostic – to avoid forming an opinion but act as if He does not exist. In reality, it is not logical at all. That is not the way we run our affairs in life. We do not hold back actions until all facts are known and proven beyond doubt. Most of the decisions we make in life are based on past experiences and probabilities. For example, sustaining our life and health is a serious matter, but there is hardly any health matter about which we do not encounter strongly differing views among researchers. We follow the view held by most professionals and take precautions or medications accordingly. An agnostic attitude in health matters will be to reject every advice and to refuse any check up, precautions, or treatment until a person himself is able to prove validity of the generally held opinion. Thus, when something very valuable is at stake, agnosticism is not logical. Risk aversion and protection from danger is logical.

Considering the consequences of their attitude, agnostics are, for all intents and purposes, in the same boat as any other disbelievers such as atheists. They are taking the same huge risks with their future and missing out the same astounding payoffs for a paltry benefit in this world. Agnosticism can be acceptable only for a very brief temporary period when a person is trying to figure out which way to go. But living a life like an agnostic for any longer period is in fact worse because it is a cop-out, an abdication of responsibility to oneself and carelessness in an area that is the most important aspect of one's life in terms of the duration of consequences and permanence of the impact.

The behaviour of atheists and agnostics can be explained by the example of the large-scale forest fires that have recently raged in Australia, California or Canada, which engulfed residential communities and in which many people lost their homes. As the wind patterns were changing and new communities were endangered by fire, authorities were sending representatives to warn the inhabitants of the impending danger so that they could get ready to vacate the area on short notice. The Creator did the same thing. He sent his representatives to warn people of the impending danger of the Fire of Hell. Atheists are those who, when warned of danger, look out of their window and see the green trees and feel the breeze of the wind and say: That is false propaganda, I do not see any fire or its trace. An agnostic hears the warning, hears the atheist's comment and decides not to do anything. He cannot decide between the conflicting opinions and cannot be bothered to go out and research the credibility of either of the claims. He has no time to assess the reality of the situation because he is busy watching television and playing games. Both (the atheist and the agnostic) want to wait until they can see the fire from their window, but that might be too late. Another example will be that of tropical storms during hurricane season. The weather people warn about the impending danger of the ferocious storm of category four or five that might be heading to a locality. Waiting to see it out of your window to be certain of its occurrence will definitely be too late to do anything for your safety, as atheists or agnostics want to do. In the same way, waiting for certainty before believing in Allaah will be too late because Allaah does not accept faith from a person once the reality of God and Hereafter becomes evident at the moment of death.

The same example can be applied to those who believe in God but not in a manner befitting His Infinity, those who do not believe in all of His messengers including the last messenger, Muhammad, or those who do not believe in obeying Him despite believing in His existence. They will not be able to attain Allaah's forgiveness and salvation because of their defective faith. They are like those who believed in the existence of the fire and followed the evacuation order, but instead of taking a direct straightforward path as prescribed, followed a different route, got lost and ended up in an area surrounded by fire instead of a safe area.

A believer listens to the warner, verifies the authenticity of the message by available means and pertinent questions, perceives the danger, packs up and leaves for safety following the route exactly as prescribed.

Hence, you should consider for your own well-being in this world and in the Hereafter to accept Allaah as your Lord, Master and Creator, to accept Islam as your way of life and to surrender to Him in obedience as a Muslim.

Chapter 8

What is Islam?[28]

THE word "Islam" is an Arabic derivative the root of which is used to connote peace, surrender, obedience, and submission. All these meanings are very significant in denoting the true nature and purpose of Islam.

The objective of Islam is to bring peace and tranquillity to individuals, human society and its surroundings through a moderate, fair, equitable, and balanced way of life that takes shape when people wilfully surrender in obedience to Allaah. Because of its comprehensive and appropriate meanings, Allaah chose this word to name the way of life (Deen) that he wanted human beings to follow. He wants people to choose a way of life that is based on obedience to Himself. A lifestyle permeated with submission to Allaah helps people to be at peace with themselves and with their environment. Hence Al Islam — the religion of Islam — means **a religion that brings peace to individuals and human society through people's obedience, servitude and submission to Allaah.**

Islam, thus defined, is the religion of the whole universe because everything in the universe is obedient to Allaah as they function exactly according to the laws of nature Allaah decreed for them.

---

[28] Based on 'Towards understanding Islam' by Syed Abul A'la Maudoodi

Islam also precisely fulfills the purpose for which human beings were created. It is Allaah's religion that He has promulgated for human beings since Adam's creation[29]. In other words, Islam is not a religion of a certain geographical area, a certain race or a certain time. It is a universal religion of the people of all time and all races. It was the religion of previous prophets and messengers (like Noah, Abraham, Moses, and Jesus). They all basically lived Islamic lives in obedience to Allaah and called everyone in their societies towards Islam — submission and surrender to Allaah.

Islam is called "The Straight Path" because, according to Allaah and His messengers, it is the only direct, straightforward and safe path that takes people away from the fire towards safety and salvation.

Who Is a Muslim?

Anyone who believes in and acts according to Islam is a Muslim. Hence a Muslim is a person who submits to Allaah in servitude and who, by following His commandments, lives a balanced life that makes him at peace with himself, his society and his environment.

The word "Muslim," in this way, is an attributive title. It can be applied to persons or entities. When this definition of Muslim is applied to entities, everything in the universe can be called Muslim. The laws and commands of Allaah (usually termed as the laws of nature) are followed consistently by every entity in the universe without fail. For example, given any circumstances, matter behaves consistently

---

[29] "With Allaah, the only Deen (religion and way of life) is Islam."…"So do they seek other than Allaah's Deen (religion and way of life), while to Him have submitted everything in the heavens and earth (the whole universe), willingly or unwillingly; and to Him they will be returned?"…"Whoever seeks a Deen (religion and way of life) other than Islam, it will not be accepted from him, and he will be among the losers in the Hereafter." The Qur'aan 3:19, 83, 85

according to its properties. It expands when heated and contracts when cooled. Similarly, the heavenly bodies rotate and revolve at the speed, direction and the orbit destined for them. Plants grow and bear their fruits according to the laws of nature. Animals follow their instincts throughout their life. In this way, all these creations are Muslim because they are obeying the commands of Allaah ordained for them in the form of physical or natural laws or instincts. They have been created to obey the law of Allaah prescribed for them. Their not having a choice to disobey ensures that they always follow all the rules consistently. The only reasons human beings have been able to progress and gain benefits from research in physical sciences is because all the elements and entities in nature consistently obey Allaah, or in other words, remain Muslim (obedient) to him.

By the definition of Muslim given above, every human being, even an atheist, is physically Muslim. Our life is sustained only because every cell of our body continues to function exactly as Allaah set the rules for it to function. When we willingly adopt obedience to Allaah in the aspects of life in which we have the freedom to make choices, we become close to our nature and our surroundings, experiencing harmony and balance with our physical environment.

Also by this definition, any human being of any time and any place who commits himself or herself to the servitude of Allaah by adopting the Islamic way of life is a Muslim. People like Adam, Noah, Abraham, Moses, and Jesus were Muslims because they all followed the commandments of Allaah in perfect obedience to Him; they believed in their fellow prophets and messengers; and they promoted accountability in the life Hereafter. Similarly, the committed, sincere followers of these prophets were also Muslims because they obeyed Allaah as they were told to obey Him.

The connotations of "obedience to Allaah" and "attaining and keeping peace" represented by the word Muslim are so significant that Muslims do not like the mispronunciation or misspelling of this word, as is done by many people and organizations in the West out of ignorance. Any variation in pronunciation such as pronouncing "s" as "z" or any variation in spelling such as "Moslem" (instead of Muslim) is unacceptable for Muslims as the misspelled or mispronounced word loses the real meaning.

Because followers of religions like Buddhism and Christianity deify their main religious personalities and they name their religions after the names of those founding personalities, people sometimes use the term Muhammadanism for Islam or Muhammadan for Muslim. These are invalid terms for various reasons:

- Muslims do not believe in the divinity of Muhammad. Far from it. In fact, Muslims are very sensitive about the oneness, uniqueness and infinity of Allaah. The idea of deifying any human being, be it Muhammad or Jesus, peace be upon both of them, is repulsive to Muslim taste.

- Islam is all about Allaah. It pivots around Him, and is extremely sensitive about the role and place of Allaah in a Muslim's life. Muslims do not want to be attributed to Muhammad, a human being.

- Islam was not founded by Muhammad. It is the religion of Allaah that was followed by Adam, the first human being, and all the prophets before Muhammad.

- The name of the religion (Islam) as well as the name of the followers (Muslim) have been given by Allaah Himself[30]. Muslims do not like to replace these God-given terms by the names that have been concocted by people.

- It is only civil, ethical and polite to call someone by their proper names, i.e., Islam (the religion) and Muslims (the followers).

[30] "He named you Muslims previously as well as in this (Book)." The Qur'aan 22:78

Chapter 9

The Distinguishing Features of Islam

The Religion of Nature

ISLAM is the religion of nature because nature is obedient to Allaah fully and consistently. It is the religion of nature because it fulfills the innate quest entrenched in human nature by Allaah. Most importantly, it is the religion of nature because it is in accordance with the natural make-up of human psyche[31].

Allaah is the designer of human nature. Knowing its strengths and weaknesses, He has given us a religion which fits well with it, capitalizes on its strengths and constructively channels its weaknesses. Just as the designer of a product knows the best way to operate and get the maximum benefit out of a device, Allaah knows the best ways human beings should behave to constitute a society that will fit perfectly in its environment and flourish to be at its best. The Islamic rules and regulations given by Allaah are the rules best suited for our individual well-being as well as that of society as a whole. Islam is designed to bring out the best in people.

Man-made religions often require their adherents to defeat their nature or indulge in activities that are against the normal demands of nature. For example, they expect their followers to avoid marriage,

---

[31] "So align your face (self) uprightly toward the Deen (of Islam) — Allaah's nature on which He has created people — making no change in the creation of Allaah. This is the right Deen (religion and way of life) but most people do not know." The Qur'aan 30:30

require people to shun their worldly needs, or suggest they live a solitary life in jungles and monasteries. Islam teaches people to fulfill their natural demands in moderation without violating the rights of other people or Allaah's laws. **It strongly discourages people from trying to defeat human nature.** It positively utilizes the good aspects of human nature as well as trains people to control their bad urges. It shows us the ways to be the best while satisfying our needs in accordance with our nature.

The Religion of Peace

Islam is a religion of peace in several ways. As mentioned before, the Islamic way of life being in harmony with our nature, with our own physical make-up and with the nature of our surroundings, grants each practising Muslim inner peace and tranquillity. When an entire society practises an Islamic way of life, people in that society can enjoy the natural harmony and balance with their global environment. A society practising[32] Islam flourishes and prospers in the same manner as a plant flourishes in its own ideal environment.

In addition to providing inner peace to the individual and a flourishing atmosphere to the society, Islam also protects the physical environment of the globe. If we look at our surroundings on earth and reflect on the natural balance that had always existed among the species and ecosystems, it will be evident that if there were there no human beings, all forms of life and ecosystems would have continued to function, operate and flourish in a balanced, harmonious and sustainable way. No species of animals would have dominated other species over a long period of time, no animal would have killed or

---

[32] A society practising Islam should not be confused with the Muslim majority countries. The reason we observe problems in Mulsim countries is precisely because they do not practise Islam.

annihilated others just for fun or game, and thus no ecological disaster would have taken place. All these problems have been caused by our excesses and abuses of the freedom and dominion granted by the Creator. People abuse their freedom by transgressing reasonable limits, by indulging in excessive consumption and by being extravagant and greedy. Islam establishes peace between humans and the environment by making humans responsible users of God-given resources to fulfill only their needs in moderation. Not only does Islam teach these principles, but it also warns people of their accountability on the Day of Judgment for the waste or extravagant use of natural resources.

Islam also establishes peace within human society itself. Peace in a society is disturbed only in cases when someone:

* Wants to take advantage of others;
* Refuses to honour others' rights;
* Declines to fulfill one's responsibilities;
* Tries to get more than one's share; or,
* Infringes upon other's honour, wealth or life.

These are all different forms of disobedience to Allaah. Persons who are obedient to Allaah will neither violate rights of others, nor shirk responsibilities, nor try to get even a little more than their fair share from others.

These are also different types of injustices people commit against each other. Peace is disturbed in the society by injustice and the victims' reaction to injustice. Islam is a religion of peace because it establishes justice in the society. It requires its adherents to be the active establishers of justice in the world[33]. When a society, as a whole, practises the principles of Islam (obedience to Allaah), it is permeated with peace and justice[34].

Note: footnotes for 33 and 34 are found on the bottom of the next page.

Thus, Islam establishes peace[35] within an individual, within a society, with its global neighbours, its environment, and its ecology. The point to remember here is that these benefits accrue through a consistent practice of Islam, not just a claim to be Muslim or a mere belief in Islam.

The Religion of Balance and Moderation

The whole universe is governed by and is operating on the principle of balance and equilibrium. Allaah wants people to adopt balance

---

[33] O believers, be determined practitioners of justice as witnesses for Allaah's sake, even though it be against yourselves, or your parents, or near relatives; whether it concerns rich or poor. Allaah is more considerate of both of them. Therefore do not follow a passion or desire lest you lose the balance. And if you distort it or disregard it, then surely Allaah is well-aware of what you do." The Qur'aan 4:135

Thus, the believers must practise blind justice in their personal dealings and also be the determined activists to establish the system of justice –Islam – in their societies. Even if the demands of justice go against one's personal interests or those of their closest relatives, justice must be served. The blind practice of justice, regardless of who is involved, rich or poor, wil be in the interest of everyone in the long run. Similarly, complete implementation of Islamic teachings will also create a balanced and just society where rights of 'haves' and 'have-nots' are optimally cared for. True believers should never let their feelings, biases, and desires of favouring certain people or their passion for certain groups or causes ever come into their way of practising justice. Finally, people have been warned that Allaah is watching them, is fully aware of all their intents and actions, and will hold them accountable if they:

• try to twist the facts to validate/qualify their decision;

• ignore the principle of justice in their dealings with people.

Also:

"O believers, stand out firmly for Allaah, as witnesses for justice, and let not hatred of a people incite you not to act equitably. Be just, that is nearer to piety. Observe your duty to Allaah; surely Allaah is well-aware of what you do." The Qur'aan 5:8

Thus, neither love nor hate for anyone should come in the way of establishing justice.

---

[34] The purpose for which Allaah sent guidance was: "So that people maintain (their affairs) with justice." The Qur'aan 57:25

---

[35] The Book has come to you "By which Allaah guides those who pursue His pleasure to the ways of peace." The Qur'aan 5:16

and moderation as well. Human beings, however, when left on their own, without guidance from Allaah, tend to go to extremes. When the disadvantages and problems created by one extreme are realized, people go back all the way to the other extreme without stopping in the middle. This vicious circle never ends. As history is witness, human beings cannot attain balance on their own[36]. They need divine guidance to find the balancing point.

On issues relating to the social sciences, Islam stipulates a balanced position that people should follow. Examples abound. On any issue, the Islamic proposition will be found to be a superb example of balance and moderation. For example:

- The Islamic propositions about God, creation, prophets, etc., as described herein before, are most sensible and in-between extremist positions.

- **Jews reject Jesus completely. Christians deify him. Islam puts him in his legitimate, respectable position of being a messenger of Allaah sent with astounding miracles.**

- Religion usually considers sex anti-spiritual, looks down upon it and promotes celibacy or devises such restrictive rules about marriage and divorce that social life starts to suffocate. In reaction to it, Western society went to the other extreme and we see that that sexual gratification has been aggrandized and it knows no rules or bounds. This attitude has weakened the family unit and threatened the very fabric of society. Islam teaches a very balanced and moderate stance that does not consider marital sex counter spiritual (in fact, it encourages conjugal relations between spouses), allows appropriate flexibility in marriage and divorce rules, outlaws extramarital sex, and strengthens the family as a fundamental social unit of society.

---

[36] This point is further elaborated in other writings of the author.

It is amazing to visualize how balanced and well proportioned a person's life and human society become when Islam is completely followed in its pure form. Just as ecosystems undisturbed by human intervention have a natural harmony and balance, human beings can enjoy similar harmony and balance within their own society when they practise an Islamic way of life.

The Original Religion

Islam is the original religion that was promulgated by Allaah for the whole universe including humankind. It was the religion for which human beings were created and it was the religion taught to the first human couple, Adam and Eve. All other religions are the corrupted or distorted forms of the original Islam. These distortions usually happen through heresies. It was through heresies that Islam taught by Moses became Judaism and Islam taught by Jesus became Christianity.

Whenever people's innovations and interpretations changed the face of Islam, Allaah sent a prophet or messenger to re-present, demonstrate and propagate the true religion, the pure form of Islam, just as it happened during the period between Moses' departure and Jesus' advent. This process had continued throughout human history until the last prophet, Muhammad, peace be upon him, was sent. Prophet Muhammad brought the last, most perfect and final edition of Islam for all people until the end of the world. That version of Islam is fully preserved. Even if the followers of Islam do not properly practise the religion, it is still available in its pristine pure form to everyone interested.

The Religion of Human Equality

Islam very strongly and emphatically asserts that all human beings are from a single pair of first human beings. They are all relatively similar in terms of potential, psychology, conscience, urges, desires, lusts, inclination to do good, propensity to do bad, and so on and so forth. There is no such thing as nobility, royal blood, super race, superior genealogy, or a preferred line. The birth of a person in a particular family, clan, tribe, nation, or race does not mean anything to Allaah and it must not carry any special rights, privileges, status, or allowances, nor must it entail any disadvantage, liability, derogation, or social handicaps. Allaah does not play favourites on the basis of genealogy. To Him all human beings are the same and must be treated the same. The only factor that makes a difference is how an individual fulfills the objective for which Allaah created human beings: total obedience to Allaah. Their performance as Muslims and the quality of their obedience is the only criterion that differentiates people[37]. This quality of performance cannot be and is never inherited. It is completely individual. Hence all definitions of classes and all discriminations on the basis of race, colour, ethnic origins, languages, etc. are repugnant to Islamic taste.

Not only does Islam strongly assert the equality of human beings, but also is it the only religion that effectively and practically puts an end to discrimination. It brings the whole of humanity to the same level playing field, differentiating between them only on the basis of whether a person is obedient or disobedient to God. The Prophet Muhammad and his companions elevated the slaves and the downtrodden to lead the so-called "noblest of the nobles," and thereby practically and effectively the idols of race and nobility were broken. The biography of the Prophet and the early history of Islam are replete with examples unmatched by any other religion, culture or civilization thus far.

---

[37] "O people! Certainly, We created you from a male and a female and made you clans and tribes only to enable you to recognize one another. The most honourable of you to Allaah is the most pious of you." The Qur'aan 49:13

The Global Religion

Theoretically, Islam is not restricted to people of a certain tribe, race, colour, or geography. Neither is it eastern or western, nor northern or southern. It is a universal religion for all races of all lands. Similarly, the term Muslim, as defined and described earlier, is an attributive title that transcends the constraints of time, space, lineage, ethnicity, and physical features of human beings. Any person during any time in any geographical region belonging to any section of humanity who decides to obey Allaah, as He wants to be obeyed is a Muslim.

Even practically, Muslims are a universal people. Their identity cannot be linked to any segment of geography. They belong to all of the first, second and third world countries. They hail from all eastern, western, northern and southern regions. They come in every tone and colour of the skin, hair and eyes; they speak all languages; they wear all kinds of clothes; and they reside in almost every part of the world. In other words, Islam is the religion of blacks, whites, browns, and yellows living in almost every corner of the globe and every continent of the earth. It is estimated that there are more than one billion Muslims in the world, and Islam is considered to be the fastest growing religion on the earth.

The Liberating Religion

Allaah created human beings free, requiring them to accept only one bondage, i.e., slavery and servitude to Allaah Himself. When people and societies move away from subservience to Allaah (Islam), they end up submitting to a variety of subjugations, bondages, slaveries, and servitudes. Ordinary people are enslaved by the machinations of leadership, by the stranglehold of clergy (priests, ministers, rabbis, mullahs), by the brainwashing of propagandists and strategists, by economic bondage of an extremely powerful capitalist super class, and by the overwhelming influences of heroes, stars and celebrities. Those who have any kind of power and influence are in bondage to their own insatiable ambitions, greed, power hunger, and desire for control. Almost all non-religious and many so-called religious people are shackled by lusts, temptations, fantasies, and the never-ending quest for maximizing their narrowly defined worldly pleasures and materialistic consumption.

When a person decides to submit to Allaah with the proper understanding and commitment to Islam, he or she is freed from all of these slaveries, bondages and shackles. Islam changes their paradigm about life and their outlook towards the world. This changed outlook of having Allaah as one's only Lord and the Hereafter as one's ultimate goal is so redeeming and liberating that a believer feels an immense relief and freedom. And it is not merely a feeling — true believers do only what they feel is appropriate and is pleasing to Allaah, regardless of what people of power and influence dictate or what their own lusts and desires demand.

The Most Tolerant and Inclusive Religion

Islam has been the prescribed way of life for all of humanity from the beginning of time. Various prophets and messengers who came were all Muslims and their true followers were also all Muslims. From Adam to Muhammad, it is all one series and one brotherhood. Adam, Noah, Abraham, Ishmael, Isaac, Jacob, Joseph, Moses, Aaron, Job, David, John, Jesus, and Muhammad were all brothers and so were their followers. This brotherhood includes a host of other prophets and messengers whose names have not been mentioned but who were sent to different parts of the world at different times[38]. There is no reason for any animosity against any of them or among them. That is the Islamic view. Islam goes one step further and makes it a requirement that every Muslim must believe in every prophet of Allaah who was sent to mankind. Every Muslim respects and loves all of the prophets that have been mentioned. Is there any other religion with that kind of positive attitude, that much tolerance and that vast inclusion?

To indicate his relationship to earlier prophets, the Prophet Muhammad gave an example of a well-built, superb building that had a corner stone missing. People saw and marvelled at its beauty, craftsmanship and design but wondered about the empty spot of the missing stone. Then he said, "I am that corner stone." With the coming of Prophet Muhammad, the marvellous house of the prophethood has been completed.

Naturally, not all claimants who have or who claim to follow these noble prophets are genuine in their claim. And that includes the claimants who claim to follow any of the prophets including Muhammad. That is where the line is drawn – the truly obedient believers versus others who just follow their own lusts, desires and biases while claiming to be believers. True followers of the prophets are included in this universal brotherhood of Islam; others are excluded. Even in that exclusion, the matter has to be treated like that of a family. That is, some members of the human family have walked away from the path of the family. They need to be counselled and reconciled back into the family. If they still want to remain estranged, it is their prerogative. This idea of reconciling back into the

---

[38] "Indeed, We have revealed to you (O Muhammad) as We revealed to Noah and the prophets after him. And We revealed to Abraham, Ishmael, Isaac, Jacob, the Descendants, Jesus, Job, Jonah, Aaron and Solomon, and to David We gave the Psalms. And (We sent) messengers about whom we have narrated (their stories) to you and about whom We have not narrated to you." The Qur'aan 4:163-164

family is one of the reasons that those who come back to Islam are not called "converted," rather they are called "reverted" because they have reverted back to their nature and their original way of life.

Islam – A Way of Life

When it comes to religion, people think of it as a set of rituals, sacrificial rites or incantations that are performed to please a deity so that the deity can help the worshippers in their needs and desires. **Islam is not a religion in that sense at all.**

Throughout our discussion, we have taken "religion" to mean the philosophy of life by which people live and the paradigm through which people look at the world. Islam is a religion in that sense. But, as it may have been evident from the points made so far, it is even more than that. It is a complete way of life. It is the way the real Muslims think and act. It is the way they make their decisions and choices. It is the way they set their priorities and determine their goals. It is the way they spend their nights and days and run their lives.

Islam encompasses every aspect of one's personal life: career, business, family, economic, social, political, moral, cultural, leisure, and spiritual. It also governs the collective affairs of the community of believers whether it is to do with economic policy, social policy, political system, penal code, judicial system, diplomacy, foreign policy, defence, or international relations.

In brief, Islam is a "Deen," a comprehensive way of life, for individuals as well as for the community (state) — a way of life that is centred on total obedience to and passionate love for Allaah. In adopting the Islamic way of life, a Muslim's individual objective is to please Allaah by excelling personally in this world for the success in the Hereafter; the objective of the community is to have the most caring, sharing, just, equitable, peaceful, balanced, and moderate society.

The collective mission of the Muslims was well described by Raba'y bin 'Aamir in the following words, when asked about it by an Iranian commander:

To liberate those who so wish, from the bondage and servitude of human beings by introducing them to the servitude of Allaah; to free them from the tight confines of this world by expanding their outlook towards its immense dimensions; and, to redeem them from the tyranny of their lifestyles and religions by means of the equitable balance and moderation of Islam.

SUMMARY

ISLAM is the original, natural, most inclusive, liberating, comprehensive, and complete way of life, and it was taught, preached and practised by all of the prophets and messengers. It is based upon some logically sound and rationally sensible beliefs such as the following:

- *This universe and everything in it, including human beings, has been created by Allaah, the Creator, the Master and the Lord of the universe as well as of human beings. He is One, Unique and Infinite. He was worshipped by Adam and all the prophets and messengers and their true followers.*

- *Everything in the universe is obedient to Allaah and has no choice but to follow His commandments that are usually described as "laws of nature." Physically, the human body is subject to the commands of Allaah as are all other living things. But behaviourally, human beings have been given freedom of choice.*

- *Although human beings have been given the freedom to make decisions about their way of life, they should choose to submit to the commands of Allaah and to follow the Islamic way of life.*

- *The commands of Allaah and Islam were brought to us by some chosen human beings called Prophets or Messengers (of Allaah) such as Noah, Abraham, Moses, David, Jesus, and Muhammad, peace be upon them. Muhammad (peace be upon him) was the last of such Messengers. Allaah's commands brought by earlier prophets were contained in books like the Torah, the Psalms, and the Gospels. The subsequent miscoding and misinterpretation of their teachings caused their followers to drift away from Islam. The Word of Allaah, as revealed to Muhammad (peace be upon him) is contained in the Holy Qur'aan, the text of which has been fully preserved beyond a doubt. Islam in its pure form is thus available to all seekers of the truth.*

- *If people choose to adopt Islam in this life, they will be at peace with themselves, their nature, their society and their environment. Moreover, they will be rewarded in the life Hereafter in the Gardens of Paradise. If they choose to follow their own whims and man-made ideologies, they suffer imbalance, problems and discontentment in this life and will be punished for disobedience in the Hereafter.*

- *The important thing is to choose the path of obedience (Islam). Although people are not perfect and they will make mistakes regardless of how good they are, that does not mean they will all end up in Hell or that they should give up trying. Allaah is forgiving, kind and merciful to all those who keep trying their best to remain on the path of obedience. He will admit them into paradise by His Grace because of their sincere devotion and constant efforts. The key is a consistent, determined effort to practise Islam, not just a "claim" to be Muslim.*

If the points, logic and rationale presented herein make sense, you owe it to yourself to accept Allaah as your Creator, Master and Lord and to submit to Him as a Muslim. If the matter is not yet clear for you, please re-read it and reflect on the unclear points. In case you have questions about the rationale presented here, please feel free to discuss them with the author.

Please remember that your reaction to this invitation has an eternal impact on your future. Your personal success depends on it. You cannot afford to take it lightly or ignore it without making a decision. Please do not let other people make a decision for you by default. Please make a decision that you can live with and be comfortable in justifying to your Creator on the Day of Judgment.⚜